No Place F

Maudlin Heart

No Place for The Maudlin Heart

Rosamund Stanhope

PETERLOO POETS

First published in 2001
by Peterloo Poets
The Old Chapel, Sand Lane, Calstock, Cornwall PL18 9QX, U.K.

© 2001 by Rosamund Stanhope

**A catalogue record for this book is available
from the British Library**

ISBN   1-871471-92-3

Printed in Great Britain By
Antony Rowe Ltd, Chippenham, Wilts.

ACKNOWLEDGEMENTS

Acknowledgements are due to the editors of the following in which some of these poems appeared for the first time: *Anglo/Welsh Review, London Welshman, Outposts, Pennine Platform, Poetry Review, Poetry Wales, The Rialto, S/E Wales Dial-a-Poem, Spectrum, Wayfarers.*

southwest arts

To Louise and Ben

Contents

Shangri La

Never here the risk of
the missed catch, the lost
'bus, the possibility of the
bottom falling out of the
lotus-market; the certainty that
the face we love will be no longer
there; that one day all this Noddy stuff will dissolve
and Andy Pandy suffocate in his dream-box.

On this island the sun casts no
shadows; amaranth survives without
rain; no fly in the
appointments, chloramine in the
water; no valley in our
alley.

And therefore no
pungent hush as the shower comes down
to rescue the fifth
Test; no final poignant kiss
on the cold cheek of the
dead; just the usual boring
immortelles, the assurance of
helichrysum, the illimitable Tithonus dawns.

The Grass I Meant to Swale

The grass I meant to swale,
when work stands still
mouths its green millions to a soul;

the flower I meant to cut,
when the task is quiet
counts its green thousands to a shoot;

the time I meant to spend
on the prodigal round
clinks its gold moments in my hand.

So out of time I hold
the ticking world
whose every chime is gold

and out of work I spell
the countless miracle
the blade and the bell

and in my acute design
leave blunter men
to ply the indelicate hone,
to scythe the overgrowing lawn.

The Jetty

I remember it as a private
region where people those days hardly ever came
to put cars away;
high brick walls, doors, a rarely-observed
aspect of houses, like one's profile
seen unexpectedly in a mirror, an ulterior
impression, as if observed in thought.

In common with all such
locations existing beyond habit
its Victorian coach-houses
converted to garages were drenched with the
timeless ethos of places seldom visited
so that this cul-de-sac
echoing with the occasional
sound of a horn

caught a tincture of the
singularity which Cortes must have felt
confronted by the abrupt
gaze of the Pacific
and all Estremadura forgotten behind him.

Freeholders

I find them in offshore moments, recognise
the tiddly suit, Number One
square rig, category badge
crown, killick, doeskin, braid.

They are indemnified
against searches, contracts, saving clauses
premiums, property
of a terminable, hazardous or wasting nature,
actions, costs, claims, demands.

For they inhabit
houses of sandstone shale and basalt
gardens of dulse and bladder-wrack
oar-weed and purple laver
and have and enjoy in perpetuity
the vast freehold of the North Sea.

The Lion and the Rose

The Lion and the Rose
finials on gable and turret;
in the great hall the linen-fold,
the four-centred arch;
velvets, furs, jewels, embroideries,
Henry in his slashed
doublet writing music
to the sound of hautboy and lute.

A fine day in the suburbs; the semis
coruscating in the heat;
mums in aprons stewing
rhubarb; kids chewing
Choc bars, peanuts, Bounty;
and bells up the long street,
Mister Softee playing "Greensleeves."

Penny Black

Restrained, in irreproachably good taste
it appeared in eighteen-forty, giving rise to
hordes of German pfennig parodies – Italy's fasces,
                                        Austria's jagerhorn
over which trash the British protectorates presided
expensive, stylish, with heads of monarchs
instead of Banana presidents, photogravure impressions
of windmills, bulldogs, daisies.

It was simply, like Babycham and Lenin
the thin end of the wedge.
Aunt Jeanette, writing from Hove, averred
that Victoria would favour her chaste image
residing in mourning, but valuable, on Stanley Gibbons'
shelves;
but, my dear, it resulted in an invasion
of vulgarians, Hottentots, rabble,
and now we may even get pictures of Mtama and
Ngorongoro.

Golden Wedding

They pose in front of the
euonymus; beside the rolled gold
salver they'll never use; the ersatz
freesia with the Soir de Paris
perfume; the reprint of Flatford Mill
which they do not like.

They have given the local Press
the recipe for a happy
marriage; share the money and
the trouble; while she has misered up
the Co-op. shares to leave
to the boys; and he has larked his
dido with a fifty-year-old
little bit of fluff in a council flat.

But on this day the sunshine
lends its qualified approval to
half a century of calloused
habit; in front of friends and Aunty Mel
she hears the nightingale
from her balcony; he fights his duel
with Tybalt, and survives.

Harness Room

Bridle and bit and trace
gone from the rotting nail
a caul of cobwebs on whitewashed brick
where shadows of larch and ivy hold
a nodding conversation with the sun.

Landau and phaeton have gone
gone the bright quarrel of harness
gone the cosmetic trash and clobber
knick-knack, bibelot,
gewgaw, bauble;
gone the long peacetime picnic
when a visit to Aunt
was a clopping day's campaign.

But something stays
in this quiet room where sunlight stamps
the wide sash window on the wall
built fastnesses before
general conscription, when war
was gallant and glorious, fought
by braided toffs in some lost
kopje or remote crimea; before
Hahn and Strassman, Rutherford, Bohr.

Apple Picking

Through green leaves I pick them, the small
breasts of apples rewarding my hand.
High up, stroking the sky
they depend from sprays, they crowd the sleeves of
trees, a child's temptation.

Absolved from original
sin I close my fingers
on the virgin bud, the naive
offspring of sun and rain.

And elemental
words sing in my ears as I part the boughs:
fire and water, earth and air,
the green fingers of light
on leaves. As I pull the fruit from the tree
dusk draws its nursery curtains on
the day, stung with stars, all
Joseph and maiden.

Various, the Disseminating Eye

Various, the disseminating eye
publishes each disparate feature,
the strawberries and millinery
suburbs and extremities of nature.

Piebald, mongrel, creation's
dull miscellany, its lumber —
ort and scrap and bric-a-brac
each in its private dark —
distracts the eye's bright chamber,
disperses vision.

There is no work, no wit
can single sight
except to cultivate
a way of looking
a beam to take in
gadfly and gillyflower
excrement, ordure
milk in the pan, cars in the street, news at the door;
no terms
for synthesis
other than one bright syllable that subsumes
all of the eye's anthologies.

In Memoriam

Edged in among
Commander Communications
VHF band radio receiver
Mucron Tablets, NPI Policies
the crossword, marriages and
continuations from page one
the moniker of
an obscure rifleman who
died of wounds at Cassino:
"Their name liveth for
evermore."

The Emigrant

His blue songs thrill
the Forum and the Pnyxian hill;
such a blue song should fall
on Sigeum or the Capitol.

September steers her ditch
from Bankside out to Chelsea reach;
such literary harmonies
are more in tune with Mincian seas.

November sours her air
from Gravesend on to Kingston weir;
the pearfalls rot
the rain is at the root;
such murder-coloured skies, such snow
in England — now!

The curd is on the core;
the blindworm and the bitten haw
stick in his throat;
the robin's love, the sparrow's wit
may celebrate the blight
from Barking flats to Margate hoe —

he wears his blue Aegean coat
he sings the winter and the woe —
those copyright
expensive songs about the poor.

At The Sea's Edge

Here at the sea's edge are
nautilus, brittle-star
horn-wrack and cuttle-bone
carapace, dead men's fingers
polyp and fern.

Impartial as the scum
the sea's long breakers
handle the numerous
orts without praise or blame
and in their green looms
weave dulse among drowned sailors.

Where is no gain or price
value or loss
the indifferent sea drowns
coral and bladder-weed
cypris and jade
reflecting in its nonchalance
a ruined God.

Fiction

The boardroom's in his pages
mahogany shifts, the chairman's subterfuges
congressional elections, the journey to Fort Scot
tracking the shark, roping the steer, beinging off
the hundred thousand deal
riding the chaparral
trading with natives, playing at pool.

But she in hers
talks of the trifling airs
nibbling, the clammy breaths fumbling
frost on the edge of spring
the protean I, grass
swallows about to disperse
and people in the house.

No Place for the Maudlin Heart

There's the Cross Keys, Felinfoel
ales, lather and brass
the Crown Stores and the steel-
works, the stack of the foundry,
the rectory pitch, the Plas,
Moriah and Sinai
and the quiet eye of water
looking round Penclawdd's shoulder.

And there, too, the stark
winch, the empty adit
the skeleton of the pit
shaft of Beily Glâs
telling of the bleak
drudge, the wearing
stint, the impaired sight
and the ruined lung.

There's no place for the maudlin
heart here; only the hard
face, the hacked vein
the black night overhead.
Yet, as I look at the view,
mine and chapel and pub invite
a greeting of the spirit which Keats knew
the utmost beauty could not be without.

Return to Bethlehem

So they trek west again
under the vast
embroidery of stars – the three men with their unsuitable gifts.

But here we have
the answer to your problem:
our Nazareth precinct providing platinum cribs
hand-made replicas in real sheepskin
of flock-watchers and advent lambs
one-piece jumpsuits in Mary blue
and Christoramas affording a spectacle through a
thirty-pence-a-time camera obscura
(which charge will be doubled on Fridays
when we raise our prices
in accordance with seasonal demand).

And in addition, beyond Manger Parade,
with the stalls advertising
crucifixes, thuribles, bijou shrouds, crowns of holly,
the West Bank guard.

Beili Glâs

It was not the association
of bugloss, cranesbill and the ubiquitous tare
or the mauve teazle, furze yellow as butter
or the quiet village seen across the water
caught Morgan with an artist's vision
made him stare;
no pastoral kicks for him –
It was the money in the seam.

Now look once more at a painter's composition:
there's the black winch, the adit and the shaft
the nettle in the cleft
of rusting brick
the willow-herb and the wind's rhetoric
over the empty face;

and Willie Harris, forced to be
home with the collier's pension and the gaze
as brittle as the gorse he'll never see.

I Went to the Woods in the Morning

I went to the woods in the morning
by the Valley of Cwm Cawlwyd
when the April leaves were shining
and the air was calm in the blood
but I found no fuel for burning.

On the crest of Carn Gwylathwyr
in the highest wind of the world
I watched the stormclouds gather
and the branches break from their hold
to the depths of Lyn Llyw water.

And I went to the plain before me
when I heard the tempest pass
where the Eagle of Gwernabwy
pecks at the seeds of the stars;
and I found in the broken grass
an armful of boughs to warm me.

Street Jewellery

Enamelled iron, they flash
their eighteen-ninety, nineteen-twenty
smiles: Ask for Golfer Oats, Skegness is so
Bracing;
Price's Nightlights, Kruschen
Salts, Harlene for the Hair;
Blue Bell Tabacco, Zam Buk, Mazawattee, Pomade
Divine;
fictions at the one and ten
a pound, twopence a whiff, threepence
a slab, immutable prices printed on.

No inflationary shifting
sands, no metric hokum, no ersatz
rannygazoo;
they write on the walls of time
the lie the present never tells
of something that was always better than
now.

The Camera

This is the moment taken before
the Lateiner bridge; the Archduke
splendid in sky-blue tunic, green plumes, gold braid
the medals not yet badged with blood
and Sophie beside him, the ostrich feathers, picture hat
her white silk dress still spotless
for the drive along the Appel Quay.

After this there'll be wine and speeches
music, the reception at the Konak
the dinner party at Ilidze –
what a lot to tell the children!
A perfect morning; and Sarajevo
bright with flags! Such warmth, such friendliness
she'd told Sunaric. And they'd soon be leaving;
Tuesday, Chlumetz, Konopischt, the rose garden, home.

We know they wouldn't; we've heard the story
a hundred times; Princip waits at the corner.
But the shutter with its power to arrest time filches
a tincture from eternity; there they sit
still on that hot June day; and the cold moment
of the camera's recapitulation even now
shakes us, abrades the heart.

Frost Work

Frond and filicale
hatch on the pane
the system, the design
of foliage and fern,

Clandestinely etched
by the moisture they exhale
scroll and sheath
rise from some bewitched
talent of the frost's breath.

And all at once
the adventitious shoot
is shaped with consequence
as frost endows
with its deliberate yes
the question, the doubt.

The Dinner Jacket Don

The dinner jacket don
perceiving through his glass
the critical analysis of the sensible world
elevating opinion to the Form
dissects his thesis on
the spontaneity of truth.

He gazes down
from his exalted place
on Vitigea (and his kith)
who slobbers up his dram
who pisses in the field
and innocently wipes his arse
on Plato's elegant Symposium.

I Heard a Horse

I heard a horse
through the spinning wheels of town
with their unspecified rush
and in that Acheron
of January slush
the hooves rang out
like certainty in doubt.
I heard a horse.

I heard a horse;
and all the world was green
and every mean
inimitable object showed
its singular I.
I heard a horse go by
like wonder on the clopping road.

Duw!

How the poet
can charm. But all that beefing
about the machine; presumably he'd be happy
shoring up cottage industries, observing
the werin figged in cobbled skins
nibbling nuts and groundsel.

And all that soup-and-fish at the
approach of interloping cultures
deploring Saesneg pretensions, the fabric
of lovely metaphors out of which he sews
his songs;
that mympwyol put-down pursuing the Saxon to
his holiday cottage in Talgarth or Aberaeyron
that boreal dirmyg, that Cymraeg
basting!
But his imagery. Duw!
There's beyond!

Dialogue is Dead

Dialogue is dead.
The green hands of your words
will not put up the swords
or break the red
impervious brigades.

Mendacious and Calumnious
deploy their shameless spies
the quick guards of the tongue
snipe the opponents down
the mouth's grenades
blast in the talker's face.

A mountain of dead speech
lies between loss and loss
and while the trite words bruise
the bright wounds teach
the lesson of the false
the traitor syllables.

A Married Name

Disguises the maiden; it may charge
comeliness with bombast, fudge
inference, fox meaning; demote sophistication
to smith or brown
even confer
citizenship of Kandy or the Saar.

At all events it is
a fraud, confusing the diathesis
of naming, muddying the stream of I
something that seldom fits
misses the butt, muffs the quarry.

Like a good wind it blows
two ways, resolving the complacent lie
its deed poll falseness, pseudo perjury
into a valuable assault
on truth, making a smith or a brown
of marx or cohen.

Song

Love that is bound has gone
with the late alchemy of stars at dawn
affirming as they die
what day's accustomed clarities deny.

Love that is lost remains
with the green advent of next season's rains
that start the trees to flower
through their impetuous, unreported hour.

In Praise of Engineers

Let us now praise engineers; for they accomplish.
Let philosophers ride in the rich thermals sustaining
ideas, objects and human perception,
classicists frolic in the flatulent skyways of
status dignitatis, arma virumque
and the niceties of the subjunctive in a quod clause,
poets take words on a conducted flight of the mind;

engineers alone deliver
the concrete end product, translate their blueprints
into artefacts of wood, metal and stone;
they investigate, clear and demolish,
measure earthworks and concrete, assess
retaining walls and pumping chambers
frames, mouldings, piling ancillaries, stays
quoins and keystones, gabions and pitching
deal with Universal beams, Universal columns, texture, proportion
British standard, Ordnance Data, Bills of
Quantity, numbering and coding
and so forth; and from these prodigies of labour

convert ethams of willowherb into
the Unité d'Habitation and the World Trade Center
reluctant minerals into the amazements of
the St Gotthard tunnel and the Gaillard Cut
hectares of waterweed
into the Rogunsky Dam and the Second Lake Pontchartrain Causeway
and, leaving theorists to contemplate their
insubstantial pageants, their cloud-capped powers, their
gorgeous fallacies,
build their castles in
Polesden Lacey or the North Circular Road.

The Bald Day Burls my Timeless Ear

the bald day burls my timeless ear
that in the chiming dark can hear
a tick in the watch of the sky

before noon stares with too much sight,
I that can stitch a quilt of light
behind the least star's eye.

I am the tree that likes the hill
and taste the gradient with my bole
I that am dumb in the fall

before the forest talks in green
and babels into bustling June
the word on the tip of the harl.

The Pear Trees

The pear trees are flush with blossom.
In September there will be a shower of fruit
falling precipitately, rotting; a warm cordial stench
and wasps coring the bruised flesh
half-buried in grass.

Within one week they fall and rot
a shower that would feed the hungry
of Ahmedabad's slums.
One year I threw away
a thousand, and left many thousand more.

The pears lie in the grass
blowsy marasmus of failure.
And I, well-schooled in futility
by the detritus of war
hope that someone will sweep them out of sight.

To Lucasta

I leave you, then, with this
last charm of the morning kiss
that feels the jolt and slither
of lives that ran together
in a railed interval
to the cock's warning bell.

My sure St. Christopher
of the thoroughfare,
where the head determines
the eyes' omens
in the spin of a skull
the groove of the tyre's heel
darts from kerb to kerb
and shocks the tilt of the globe.

So I to where you stand
wave my day's faith in your hand
fearing no less
your highway's trafRickless
stroll of pedestrian feet
down an empty street;

that you ensure the space
of clear, diverted ways
where the one sign admits
no crash of opposites
and cancelling with a code
the dodging wheels of God
rise up and walk with your bed
whilst I smile from the road.

Two Songs

The thrush singing at the green
eaves when the weather is still
is prompted by an April
pulse in the sun,
his tune
a mere reflex;
he will sing
like this when the spring
puts live slips in the brakes;
it is the nerves' conditioning.

The blind man singing down the street
asks for coins on his plate
his reasons bed and supper;
not all the spring's grass
will show green in his eyes
not all the spring air
charm his veins;
his shabby song presents
the brain's intelligence
of the heart's need and the eyes' hunger.

And so the two songs complicate
our ends and means:
the spontaneous joy from the bill
and the conscious cry for bread;
the agony of the wit
and the innate madrigal
with their questions obsess
our glib doctrines:
there are truths too various
for the ease of the soul.

View Through an Open Window

This view more than
satisfies. There is the ploughed
field like corded silk
sunlight and high cloud
the calm Mediterranean
and, inside, the chair, the wide
window-sill.

Is it the chance collage
of room and view that impresses?
there are the roofs of Cassis
the sea quiet as milk
and here the chair, the darkening
casement, the window ledge.

St. John of Avila
had a favourite posture
looking out from his cloister
to the roses and cistus and lavender
of a Castilian spring
finding in that a secession
from the darkness of a private vision.

Chained by the Skeins of the Moon

Chained by the skeins of the moon
I made straight for the sea
and received the sea's nature.
No wave impeded me
the dark leviathan
became my creature.

From Caer Dathyl's strand
along to Aber Menai
from dulse and the sea-girdle
I made with my magic hand
a noble horse to bear me
and cordwain for its bridle,

Astride my splendid steed
I sprang, as white as the spray
as mutable as water,
finding only the shatter
of the main about the weed
at the bed of the crumbling day.

Snide-eyed and Legless or the Uses of Adversity

Having conned the woman
into contravening the sole firman
he heard the voice of the boss
bawling across
the cool of the evening, cursing him above
the reboant herds, the ululant packs, the miauling
neighing, lowing, bleating, growling
squadrons of guff —
the olla podrida of duff
life; charging him to wind
on his ventrum in the dross
snide-eyed and legless, lacking ears.

But he found
a very handy office for his tongue
in the dwarf scutch where he could slide along
invisibly; hawthorn dosshouse, squats of briar
the ideal mattress for his pad;
and when the trees were bare
and the smug rail and gannet who
hadn't offended God
paddled their chilly passage through the air
he straggled happily, unseen
into his humble garrison
and slept the winter through.

Coming to Cefn Sidan

Coming to Cefn Sidan
it was high tide and in the chapels of the sea
I heard the loud hwyl of the waves
and shawls of snow were driven
across Carmarthen Bay.

And I thought of the Isle of May
rising like Jonah's whale
out of the drown
and the trailing, frail
white wink of the plane
as it ferried down.

Think of Tapper, closed in the cold cynghanedd
rush and hush of the wake;
think of Shelley now and Ophelia
and Glaucus tossed in the wreck
that beds the blind Tyrrhenian mariner;
think of us on the shore
and at the moment of out death.

I Hate Snow

I hate snow.
Don't talk to me of a blanket covering the bulbocodium
synthetic blossoms prettying the crataegus prunifolia;
I'm absorbed in
thawing out the door locks, wiping condensation
from the ignition leads, shovelling whales of frozen rain
from the garage drive.

And I deplore all that chatter about
carpets and icing. To me it's one deadpan near-absolute
on the rather intriguing distinctions of existence.
It aspires to the condition of the summum genus
and, as Hegel observed, pure being is identical with not-being.

I'm just waiting for the good Sol to resolve it where it lies
as boring as Sunday, almost as irrelative as heaven,
bringing back with him diversity, warm plates and purring pistons.
Come back, sweet
difference!

Moving House (1)

Always to leave
the green heirs of the grass
and the grandmothers of trees
the walls like love
the floors like centuries;

Always to lose
that genesis, the pear
where the green birds have their ways
and April's furniture
the nursery shoots and the garden are
going where time goes;

is always to keep
the greenest miracle
the essence in the sap
alive in the orchard soul —
all joy that flies and all
knowledge of joy that stays.

Ladders

There's something about ladders: they aspire to
windows for mending hasps or painting
sills; rescuing victims of
fire with their fifteen-storey excursions
making Le Corbusier's towers look pretty trite
passing all that concrete with the ease
of a long-distance runner.

Or helping butties up scaffolding holding hods
of bricks or mortar; in hardware stores
assisting one to get the candles and string
or, in corner shops, bismuth and soda.

But I had a ladder standing by a tree
in mid-October, the apple-picking season
a blue ladder leaning against the sky
like Jacob's ladder touching the skirt of heaven
reminding me that my reach
is still beyond my grasp
or what's a heaven for?

The Knights Move

Approximating things by sudden obliquities
is more rewarding than the forthright advances
of bishops, the square honesties of castles.

There is one way to preserve
our fortress reticence; and that is by
indirection: let rubes approach
with inelegant assaults, such as "Wotcher, chum!"
or, "Oi, cock!" Knights progress
in the delicate diagonals of
suggestion, reining in the looser qualities of
mateyness and candour;

observing rules like
not exchanging pleasantries, for instance,
from private property with someone in the road
not accepting presumptions from
persons to whom you have not been introduced
maintaining (but this is de rigueur)
a halcyon front to callers, against
the family brouhaha in the basement.

It's remarkable how such trifles
count; and, apart from there being an
inalienable look of The People
about pyknic types, you can tell
a gentleman from the way he consults
the menu, or suggests an
assignment; or abstracts your
investment — indirectly, that is.

All Day it has Snowed

All day it has snowed. White lies like a noun
on wedding-cake houses
and, siphoned by the east
wind, whales of snow wallow in ditches
cumber boughs.

Diversity, modification – snow dispenses
with these, making only
its one unqualified statement
smothering adjectives in the immense substantive
the loud autocracy of yes;

until the whispered doubt
widens, a crack in the ice, to divergence, digression
the allotropy of colour welcomes option
restores the epithet, the democracy of perhaps.

Winter Season

Now we can shake off all the superfluous
gimmicks and gewgaws; the pier
is boarded and padlocked; the ice-cream bar
and the fun-palace
have the "Closed" sign on the door.

Looking for sandwich papers in the dunes
the gulls lament
the absence of picnic scraps and garbage tins,
"Bed and breakfast" grate the swinging signs,
a blast curses the bent.

There are no gimcrack shoppers in the town
no candy-floss and chat;
the sea is frank about
its ability to drown;
all the trumpery of summer has been sold;
poor Tom's a'cold.

I Must Have Synonyms

I must have synonyms:
parallel vocables, roots, etymons, terms
to import, purport, imply, bespeak, express
the grade, gradation, shade, pitch, nuance, slant
of drift, gist, meaning, tenor, spirit, sense
I fancy, have a mind to, need, desire, want
to transmit, waft, deliver, send, convey
to another consciousness.

It is only by synonyms that we come close
approximate, approach, set in to, gain on truth
(which has no synonym, I think) – it is the way
we tell, appraise, inform acoustic organs, ears
for passage to the reason, nous, intelligence
of the mystery, crux, problem, rebus of the earth
and lighten the black holes among the stars.

The Quilted Prelates Raised their Voices

The quilted prelates raised their voices
loud in the homespun land of women;
The church's resonant devices
Declared that what is human
is most uncommon
the cunning'st pattern of excelling juices.

And Hi was born
banned by a gangling brain
to sort with strangers
fumbling in his embryo fingers
the chamber and the drain
fishing for God;
searching for some bright word
to praise his mother's motherhood.

The quilted prelates hushed their tongues
constrained by generals and garters
assented, "As St. Michael taught us…"
Whispered to august arms exporters
their cunning pattern of excelling songs.

And Lo was shot;
Flushed with the raping bullet through him
putting his summer wits to ruin
the diamond of his mind to rot;
and then the flies began their dirge
and round the corpse his children stammered
and all day long the vultures clamoured
from Camranh Bay to Gettysburg.

Turn Out the Light

Turn out the light, seeing we are wasting power,
let us explore our own internal vistas:
the voltage of the brain, the bright
impressive filaments of might
ampères of cash beyond the black resistors
and all the wattage of the inward stare.

Then burn our self-love into night
above the oil lamps of our true impressions
above the ancient candles of confessions
electrify the earth with our great glare
that darkens rooms where blind men are.
Turn out the power, seeing we are wasting light.